N[illegible] ON TONIGHT

A One-Act Comedy

by

Terry Collister

Published by:
New Playwrights' Network
35 Sandringham Road
Macclesfield
Cheshire
SK10 1QB

ISBN 086319 260 2

CAST

(In order of appearance)

Coxeley

Albert

Graham

Felicity

Miss Manley

Auberon

Mike

Girl with Ghetto Blaster

Other Girl

Vcronica

NOTHING ON TONIGHT

The play takes place in a Village Hall, the main stage represents the hall floor, the backdrop is curtains representing a small stage with a box podium beneath. A gap is required behind these curtains for characters to enter from. The podium is useful as some dialogue is delivered from here and will be better heard than on the main stage.

The curtain opens, the stage is bare apart from two chairs, centre stage left. PHIL COXELEY, about 40, glasses, tank top, shirt and tie, cords, brogue shoes, very posh, enters centre stage left. He moves to the centre of the stage and satisfies himself that he is in the middle. He then takes two exaggerated steps to his left and back, then repeats to his right. He mutters to himself "Fine Fine!". He then moves to the backdrop and peers behind the curtain and upon seeing what he wants he steps up onto the podium and disappears only to return immediately with a music stand/lectern which he places in the centre of the main stage, facing the audience. He now adopts the position of a lecturer.

He speaks and as speaking he turns as though talking to a circled audience:

COXELEY: "Ladies and Gentlemen, tonight I wish to extend your emotions and imaginations through the words and thoughts of the philosopher, the poet, the prophet, the man, John Molesworthy Crudd. *(He shakes his head, not satisfied with this)* No! *(He restarts)* Tonight gathered Cruddites. *(Pause)* No! Tonight my friends it is my privilege to bring to you the poetry, the prophesies, the pronouncements of the person John... *(All through this he is turning and addressing an imaginary circled audience. He is rudely interrupted)*

ALBERT: Oi - Hey, who do you think you are?

(A man in his early 60's enters centre stage left. He is wearing a brown overall and his hands are in the pockets)

COXELEY: Sorry?

ALBERT: I said who do you think you are? You can't just wander in here as though you owned the place, and what are you doing spinning round on my floor? Two and a half hours it took me last night to get that shine after them Badminton players *(this is said with some accentuation)* had finished. You can't leave those scuff marks overnight, you have to get at 'em straight away, I can't understand why they let 'em use this place, it's a Village Hall not a sports centre.

COXELEY: I'm sorry, I don't think I've had the pleasure.

ALBERT: That's your fault - and then they have those Whist Drives, with all them tables scratchin' the surface, and they expect me to keep the place like new. And then you come in and start spinnin' round like a top with those black rubber soles. Just what are you doin'?

COXELEY: Coxeley - Philip Coxeley. *(He offers a hand to shake, there is no response)* I'm rehearsing for tomorrow night - The Recital?

ALBERT: Tomorrow night's tomorrow night - What are you doin' 'ere now?

COXELEY: I was told the hall was not in use tonight and that I could familiarise myself with its acoustics.

ALBERT: Oh, you were were you, by who?

COXELEY: Oh a very helpful young lady on the telephone at the

Town Hall, a Miss Standing.

ALBERT: Veronica, she's at it again. If I've told her once I've told her a thousand times, leave the bookings to me, I know what's going on. When she comes home tonight she'll get the sharp end of my tongue she will.

COXELEY: Might I ask who you are?

ALBERT: Albert Standing - Caretaker. That's *Albert* not Al, not Bert and definitely not Oy you - Albert, and I says what goes on here, not our Veronica.

COXELEY: Oh sorry. Well, is it all right if I continue?

ALBERT: I suppose so, you're not doin' any harm but you'll have to put up with me checking the lights and the fire escape doors, that's why there's nothin' on 'ere tonight - I have to check 'em sometime.

COXELEY: Thank you. *(He restarts his address)*

ALBERT: Wouldn't you be better testin' it out from the stage?

COXELEY: Oh I won't be using the stage, Crudd's words must be spoken in the round, I shall recite from here with the audience assembled in a circle. *(He gestures in a circle with his hand, around himself)*

ALBERT: I can't arrange chairs in a circle, good Lord it's bad enough in a straight line, but a circle. That must contravene the Fire Regulations, everything else does so that must. I mean, how do I clip them together? No, you'll have to use the stage.

COXELEY: But the whole meaning of Crudd would be lost that way.

ALBERT: Who's Crudd?

COXELEY: That's my Recital, "The collected works of John Molesworthy Crudd". You've probably never heard of him.

ALBERT: Has anyone?

COXELEY: Ah now there you hit the answer on the head with the question, so to speak. As Cruddites, or in some circles, Cruddites say, "If unheard, is a man heard of?" or as in the words of J.M. Crudd himself, "One can only turn a deaf ear to silence".

ALBERT: Oh yes, so who was this mouldy Crudd then?

COXELEY: 'Is' my dear friend, very much is, and its Molesworthy John *Molesworthy* Crudd, he has a tent on

Dartmoor. I fell over him so to speak one day when I was musing there. He was lying in the heather contemplating cloud speed relative to ground wind velocity, I didn't see him and tripped straight over him. That was when I first gained the experience of his command of the spoken thought.

ALBERT: Oh, told you to piss off did he?

COXELEY: Er - well - yes, but it was the way he said it, such inner depth to such a small ripost, immediately I knew that here was no ordinary man, but a modern day Plato.

ALBERT: He's Roman!

COXELEY: Greek! We started talking and I was overwhelmed by his insight and command of verse,, that day I bought a bicycle and rode up to the moor every evening. I wrote down everything he said and tomorrow night's Recital evening shall be his platform. Tomorrow night I shall spread Crudd all over the world.

ALBERT: Well I'll have to have a word with Miss Manley about the seating, I'm sure it's impossible and you'll have to wear slippers if you're goin' to be spinning around all night. Mind you I suppose I could put a mat down, one of them foam things they use on kids gymnastics nights. Yes. Well, I must get on. *(He exits stage right and shouts back as COXELEY restarts his address)* And stop spinnin' round.

COXELEY: My dear friends, this evening I shall reveal to you the inner man, tonight you shall experience movement of thought, tonight you shall meet John Molesworthy Crudd, the poet, the prophet and the personification of the inanimate. Silence can only be heard when everyone is very quiet - one of Crudd's simpler profoundments.

(During the last sentence a man and a woman enter up stage left. They are dressed in tennis whites and she carries a sports bag with a Badminton racquet sticking out. The man is GRAHAM STROUD, about 40, not extremely fit, with head band, wrist bands, towel, water bottle, flat pumps. The woman is FELICITY MARSH, about 25, good looking)

GRAHAM: *(Shouting from upstage to COXELEY)* Going to be long? *(COXELEY stops and turns, GRAHAM comes down stage to him)*

COXELEY: Beg pardon?

GRAHAM: Are you going to be long. only Felicity and I have a match to play. *(He beats his racquet on his hand)*

COXELEY: No not long, but don't worry about me, carry on.

GRAHAM: We can't I'm afraid, you're the net. I mean the net goes where you are.

COXELEY: Oh, sorry!

GRAHAM: Don't worry, you carry on while we get set up.

COXELEY: I was told the hall would be empty tonight.

GRAHAM: Yes it is, but we couldn't make it last night, commitments, and if we don't play before Saturday we'll both be eliminated. Veronica said we'd have no trouble tonight - nothing booked.

COXELEY: Miss Standing?

GRAHAM: Yes.

COXELEY: She's very helpful isn't she?

GRAHAM: Yes, and understanding - not like some I know.

COXELEY: You mean her Father?

GRAHAM: If the cap fits!

FELICITY: Come on Graham! We promised June and Gerry we'd meet them at nine in the Swan, it's a quarter to eight now.

GRAHAM: I'm sorry Felicity, I'll just find the net. *(Through curtains centre)*

FELICITY: *(Moving down to COXELEY)* Hi!

COXELEY: *(Who was about to restart)* Oh hullo, er, Coxeley, Philip Coxeley. *(He again offers a hand for shaking, it is again refused. FELICITY turns and looks upstage)*

FELICITY: Oh where is Graham? *(She calls)* Graham, Graham! *(She moves down stage right)*

GRAHAM: *(Poking his head through the curtains)* It's not here!

FELICITY: What?

GRAHAM: The net, it's not here, Rodney must have taken it home with him *(he comes downstage)* I remember he said it needed a bit of repair, he must have decided tonight was a good time to do it.

FELICITY: Well we can't possibly play without a net, and that leaves us with practically an hour to kill!

GRAHAM: Yes it does, doesn't it? What can we possibly do for an hour? *(He looks at her full in the face)*

FELICITY: Yes what. *(Hesitantly)*

GRAHAM: *(Taking hold of her hand)* Yes what? *(He takes her other hand. They stare into each others' eyes)* The gymnastics store!

FELICITY: The gymnastics store! *(They exit off stage right holding hands. COXELEY watches with gaping mouth, ALBERT appears through the curtains)*

ALBERT: Not doing much, I think your audience is going to be very bored if you're just going to stand there with your mouth open and no words coming out. *(COXELEY attempts to speak and gestures to off stage right but can't get any words out)* At least you're not spinnin' round and round anyway, but I'm not going to take any chances - I'll get one of those mats for you from the gymnastics store, you can try it out. *(He goes to exit stage right)*

COXELEY: *(Suddenly realising) NO!*

ALBERT: *(Stopping and turning)* What?

COXELEY: I need some help. *(Hesitantly to himself)* What am I doing?

ALBERT: Help?

COXELEY: Yes could you pretend to be an audience for me for a couple of minutes, it's my nerves you see, it'll help calm me down having an audience, even a pretend audience.

ALBERT: I haven't got time to be pretend audiences, got too much to do.

COXELEY: Please. *(He dashes to the chairs, gets one and places it at the opposite side of the stage)* If you could just sit in one of these. *(ALBERT goes to sit in the chair centre right, COXELEY grabbing him)* No, this one please. *(He moves him to the other chair)* Right! *(A bit panicky)* the words of J.M.Crudd. *(He starts and shouts into stage right wing away from where ALBERT is sitting)* Doing what comes naturally can catch you *OUT*, *BEWARE* the *CARE-TAKER* of desire who guards our souls and seeks amongst us when we least expect it. He would pull from under us our bed and use it as a *MAT* and that would leave us both with faces red though anger would be his alone.

ALBERT: Oi, I'm over here, what are you shouting over there for? *(He stands)*

COXELEY: *(Shouting and turning to ALBERT) WHAT?*

ALBERT: *(Shouting)* What are you shouting over there for?

COXELEY: *(Shouting)* Was I? Oh yes, just testing the vocal bounce. *(He turns away from ALBERT again and shouts)* Can you hear me all right?

ALBERT: Of course I can hear you!

COXELEY: *(Shouting even louder)* Could you hear me in the gymnastics store?

ALBERT: *(Shouting)* I could hear you down at the Town Hall, but what are you worried about the gymnastics store for? You going to put some of your audience in there are you?

COXELEY: *(Still shouting)* No but if you went there to get a *RUBBER MAT* as you were *ABOUT TO DO* this is probably how loud I'd need to shout for you to hear me isn't it?

ALBERT: But I haven't gone so you don't need to shout do you?

COXELEY: *(Shouting)* No!

ALBERT: *(Shouting)* Then shut up!

COXELEY: *(Calming down)* Oh yes!

ALBERT: Are you barmy?

COXELEY: *(To himself)* A little I think. *(To ALBERT)* It's good for you.

ALBERT: What is?

COXELEY: Shouting - clears the bronchils, gets more air into the lungs, Crudd always says shout twice a week, it helps you speak, and thrice is nicc.

ALBERT: *(Staring straight at COXELEY)* You are barmy. I'll go and get that mat. *(COXELEY grabs him and sits him in the other chair, right)*

COXELEY: Please this is very important, your help here will be invaluable. *(With his hands on ALBERT's shoulders he shouts over the top of his head)* Get out! Get out! Your deeds will be discovered, he comes the one that guards the door and locks the cupboards. He comes and you should not be there. Get out! Get out! Beware!

ALBERT: *(Pushing COXELEY off)* Oi! *(He stands)* If that's

how you're goin' to carry on I feel sorry for those in the front row. *(FELICITY and GRAHAM dash on, up right, adjusting their clothes. COXELEY is about to push ALBERT down again, he sees them, stops and says very calmly to ALBERT)*

COXELEY: Thank you, weren't you going for a mat? *(ALBERT scratches his head, shakes it and exits down right)*

ALBERT: Barmy, they always are these illiterate types - barmy! *(GRAHAM and FELICITY look sheepish)*

GRAHAM: *(From up stage)* Thanks! *(COXELEY sinks into a chair and takes out a handkerchief with which he mops his brow. FELICITY and GRAHAM advance to COXELEY)*

COXELEY: I wonder why I did that, I don't know what came over me, I've never done anything like it before.

GRAHAM: Probably not had the call before.

COXELEY: I'm quite exhausted.

GRAHAM: Me too! *(He sits in other chair)*

FELICITY: *(Left standing)* Ahm - Graham.

GRAHAM: *(Standing with a start)* Oh - sorry Felicity. *(Their eyes meet again)*

FELICITY: Still a lot of time to kill.

GRAHAM: Loads! *(They hold hands again)* Have to find something to do.

FELICITY: Have to.

GRAHAM: Gym store out of bounds.

FELICITY: Out of bounds!

GRAHAM: Play school room! *(They dash off stage left. COXELEY watches with open mouth)*

COXELEY: *(In a daze)* Oh no. *(He stands)* I need a glass of water. *(Takes lectern off up left. A women's voice is heard coming from behind the curtains)*

MISS MANLEY: Hullo, Mr Standing are you there? *(She pokes her head through the curtains, she is middle aged, slightly plump and not fashionable. She runs the local Amateur Dramatic Group, ALBERT is putty in her hands, she speaks back into the stage)* He's around here somewhere, never leaves the place, come and see the hall. *(She steps down to the main stage. She is followed by an elegant well groomed man, they stand looking around)* It's not very large but the acoustics are marvellous and with those side window curtains closed you get a perfect blackout. *(The man paces about surveying the scene, he sniffs hard)* It's the pig farm at the end of the village I'm afraid, it doesn't happen very often only when the winds in a certain direction, our audiences are quite used to it now! *(The man turns around a few times, then standing facing out he quotes in a very poetic manner)*

AUBERON: "Shall I compare thee to a summer day
Thou art more lovely and more temperate
Rough winds do shake the darling buds of May
And summers lease hath all to short a date".
(He stops and still looking out says...)
Adorable, quite adorable and so quaint.

(MISS MANLEY breathes a sigh of relief)

MANLEY: You like it?

AUBERON: Victoria it is an oasis within the desert of life's vulgarities, a tranquil haven crying out for the touch of Auberon Darling.
My Othello shall colour the walls!
My Macbeth will haunt the passageways!
My Bottom *(Pause)* will shine like a full moon on your darkened rafters!

(He knows full well what he has said)

MANLEY: Oh yes! *(Somewhat in awe)*

AUBERON: Like it - I love it! I think we shall begin our season with something light. The Comedy of Errors don't you think? *(He paces about. ALBERT appears from stage right draped in a foam mat)*

ALBERT: Here you are, you can screw about on this as much as you like. *(He throws it down on the stage)*

MANLEY: Mr. Standing.

ALBERT: Oh - Miss Manley, where did you come from? Where's he gone. *(To AUBERON)* Who are you? *(He turns to MISS MANLEY)* I'm sorry Miss Manley, people just seem to be coming and going at their pleasure tonight, I've just been to fetch this mat for a chap so he won't scratch the floor. *(He looks about)* Where's he gone? And you arrive and another one just wanders in off the street, I can't have this, I'll get rid of him. I'm very sorry *(turning to AUBERON)* I don't know who you are or what you want but whatever it is you can't have it and I don't care what our Veronica says, I sort out things here so you'll have to go and come at a proper time when I've got my bookings pad! *(He starts to usher AUBERON out)*

MANLEY: Mr. Standing, he's with me.

ALBERT: *(Immediately stopping)* Oh I'm sorry Miss Manley, I do apologise, please forgive me, if I'd known I wouldn't...

MANLEY: That's quite all right Mr. Standing *(she guides him away from AUBERON)* I quite understand.

ALBERT: Who is he Miss Manley?

MANLEY: *(Turning to front)* Auberon Darling.

ALBERT: *(Suddenly taken aback)* What did you say Miss Manley?

MANLEY: Auberon Darling! *(To ALBERT)*

ALBERT: Oh Miss Manley at last, after all these years, at last you've let that veneer of discipline slip, at last you've let loose your true feelings. *(He advances towards her and takes her hands)*

MANLEY: *(Pulling free)* Mr. Standing!

ALBERT: Call me Albert - Victoria. Oh Victoria if you only knew how long I've waited for this, yearned, pined. I'm yours Victoria, do with me as you will.

(He takes off his overall, throws it over AUBERON and grabs hold of MISS MANLEY. At this moment GRAHAM and FELICITY re-enter up left somewhat dishevelled. They see MISS MANLEY and ALBERT embracing, AUBERON stumbling into the chairs and COXELEY entering saying...)

COXELEY: Sex mad! Sex mad! *(They look at one another, kiss and say together)*

GRAHAM & FELICITY: The changing room! *(They dash off up right)*

COXELEY: *(Seeing MISS MANLEY and ALBERT)* More of them! *(He*

holds his head and exits. AUBERON frees himself and MISS MANLEY pushes off ALBERT)

MANLEY: **Mr. Standing - what's come over you?**

ALBERT: **You called me darling for the first time - Oh Victoria!**

MANLEY: **Mr. Standing I did not call you darling, Darling is the name of the gentleman.** ***(AUBERON has taken to one of the chairs)***

ALBERT: **Oh good grief! I thought you...Oh I'm sorry Miss Manley, what must you think? Please accept my apologies, Oh dear, Oh dear!**

MANLEY: ***(Soothing)*** **That's quite all right Mr. Standing I understand what red blooded women like myself can do to men, but you must control yourself. Now let me introduce you. This is none other than Auberon Darling, the great Shakespearian actor who has graciously accepted my invitation to stage a season of the Bard's work here on our humble stage.** ***(To AUBERON)*** **This is Mr. Standing, our excellent Caretaker.** ***(AUBERON stands and with disdain*** *hands ALBERT his smock. He then offers a hand to shake, he is very limp wristed)*

AUBERON: My pleasure.

(ALBERT shakes his hand, AUBERON turns and strides away. ALBERT is left with the aftermath of the worst handshake he has ever encountered, he doesn't actually know what to do with his own hand. He eventually wipes it down his front with disgust)

MANLEY: Oh Mr. Standing this is so exciting - Auberon Darling - here! *(AUBERON is pacing about looking very professional)* Look at him, the way he moves, the way he carries himself and that voice, Oh - that voice.

ALBERT: *(With disgust)* Actors! *(He puts his overall back on and takes out a filthy rag with which he rewipes his hand and uses it to blow his nose)* Actors! *(He exits stage right taking mat with him)*

AUBERON: *(Looking into the lights)* "To be or not to be, that is the question, whether tis nobler...*(The lights go out then come back on again, ALBERT's voice is heard...)*

ALBERT: Sorry about that - just testing.

AUBERON: Whether tis nobler in the mind to suffer the slings and arrows of......*(There is a tremendous banging. ALBERT's voice is heard again off stage)*

ALBERT: Sorry about that - just testing!

AUBERON: ...of outrageous fortune or......*(A toilet is heard flushing off stage, this must be through the sound system)*

ALBERT: *(Off stage)* Sorry about that.

AUBERON & ALBERT: Just testing.

(ALBERT pokes his head through the curtains)

ALBERT: Oh by the way, that's something to remember, don't flush the backstage loo during a performance, *(he disappears, then suddenly reappears)* unless it's chamber music that is! *(He laughs and disappears)*

MANLEY: *(Crossing to AUBERON)* I'm awfully sorry about this Auberon, I don't know what's come over him!

AUBERON: Fear not dear lady, there was never yet the philosopher that could endure the toothache patiently. *(To the wings)* Goodnight, goodnight, parting is such sweet sorrow. That I shall say goodnight till it be tomorrow. *(AUBERON sweeps off and the lights flash on and off. MISS MANLEY moves to the wings stage left)*

MANLEY: Mr. Standing I really do think that was very rude of you. *(She exits taking the lectern with her, there is suddenly a lot of thumping and banging off stage. ALBERT is heard shouting...)*

ALBERT: Oi, what are you doing? You can't put that there - Oi! I said you can't put that there. *(He enters up left with a YOUNG MAN and 2 TRENDY GIRLS who are chewing gum and smoking,one is carrying a ghetto blaster which is playing. ALBERT with raised voice)* Because you can't that's why - cluttering up my stage.

MIKE: *(A disco D.J.)* We're doing a gig here on Saturday!

ALBERT: A what?

MIKE: Gig - Disco - I wanted to get set up early.

ALBERT: Well you can't, take it away and come back on Saturday.

GHETTO GIRL: We was told!
ALBERT: *(Turning to her)* What?
OTHER GIRL: We was told!
ALBERT: Told!
MIKE: Yeah, the Town Hall said it would be all right, nothin' on tonight so no problem.
ALBERT: Since when has the Town Hall been able to speak?
GIRLS: *(Together)* Oh funny! *(Mockingly)*
MIKE: Someone down at the Town Hall, on the 'phone, I've got her name here somewhere. *(He fumbles in his pockets)*
ALBERT: Don't bother, don't bother *(to himself)* I'll swing for her before long, I know who it was and she was wrong! You can't leave all that stuff here. *(Pause)* We're not insured for it.
GHETTO GIRL: She said you were.
ALBERT: *(Turning)* Well we're not - can you turn that blasted thing off! *(The Girl pointedly pushes the off button)*
OTHER GIRL: *She (with elongated she-ee)* said your insurance policy covered anything properly stored in the building *(pause) she* said, so long as it was out of sight *(pause) she* said, it'd been done before *(pause) she* said...
ALBERT: She said, she said! I don't care what she said, it's what I say that matters - and I say you can't leave it here.
MIKE: But the van's gone now.
GHETTO GIRL: And we're only in a car.
OTHER GIRL: And you can't get all the gear in a car.
GHETTO GIRL: And we can't be expected to carry it.
MIKE: I won't see the driver again until tomorrow.
OTHER GIRL: And the Town Hall said....
ALBERT: *(Shouting to heaven)* Veronica! *(He storms off up right. The ghetto blaster is turned back on. The girl puts it down on the chair up left and wanders round, she turns and speaks to OTHER GIRL)*
GHETTO GIRL: Worra dump. Eh Micky why can't you get some of the better gigs, y'know in them posh hotels.
MIKE: *(Who has been foraging around looking for something)* I dunno, must be me aftershave, eh there's no sockets

ere, aw that means borrowing Kenny's extension lead, *again (he imitates an effected effeminate voice)* Oh you will look after it won't you Mickey darling *(he starts to mince about the stage)* you know I only lend it to you because you're so careful. *(At this moment AUBERON enters and sees MIKE)*

AUBERON: Oh what delightful music *(it isn't - he goes straight to MIKE and offers his hand)* Auberon darling *(MIKE shakes his hand then repeats ALBERT's reaction as AUBERON moves across the stage)* Isn't this a delightful little place? *(He returns to MIKE)* Are you a regular here? *(On seeing AUBERON, MIKE grabs the tape, switches it off and holds it in front of himself)*

MIKE: *(In a very 'macho' voice)* No, I'm just setting up for the disco on Saturday - er *(he is starting to panic)* this is Charlene and Marilyn my - *Girl*friends!

AUBERON: Ooh, two, who's lucky then? You must have something special. *(The GIRLS are giggling)*

MIKE: No! No! not really, nothing, not really, just....

AUBERON: Oh I can see this chat being very interesting, perhaps we should have a boy's get-together.

MIKE: No, that's okay. I'm very *un*interesting really *(he puts the tape back on the chair and backs off towards the stage)* boring in fact *(yawning)* tiresome *(he stumbles backwards onto stage and stands up quickly)* Excuse me! *(He vanishes behind the curtains)*

AUBERON: Oh what a pity! *(He follows after him)* I'm sure you're being too hard on yourself. *(The TWO GIRLS sit down giggling, move chair down right to left, GRAHAM and FELICITY enter, GRAHAM is carrying the Badminton net and stands)*

GRAHAM: Who would ever have expected to find it there, I mean who in their right mind would put it in the boiler room! *(To the GIRLS)* Oh hullo, waiting for someone?

GHETTO GIRL: Could be!

OTHER GIRL: Yeah!

GRAHAM: Only you can't just sit here out of the cold.

GHETTO GIRL: We're with the disco!

FELICITY: Disco?

OTHER GIRL: Yeah!

FELICITY: What disco?
GHETTO GIRL: Soundaround.
FELICITY: Soundaround?
OTHER GIRL: Yeah!
GRAHAM: Where?
GHETTO GIRL: Here.
FELICITY: Here?
OTHER GIRL: Yeah!
GRAHAM: But where?
GHETTO GIRL: Back there.
FELICITY: Back there?
OTHER GIRL: Yeah!
GRAHAM: The disco?
GHETTO GIRL: Yeah.
OTHER GIRL: Yeah!
GRAHAM: Hold on! Let's start again.
GHETTO GIRL: If you want!
GRAHAM: You are with a disco that is here but back there?
OTHER GIRL: Yeah!
GRAHAM: Back where?
GHETTO GIRL: There.
GRAHAM: *(Turning to FELICITY)* What makes me think this is a lost case? *(He goes to start again)* There is a dis....
MIKE: *(Backing onto stage from down right with AUBERON pacing him)* No, you see I'm just with the disco, it's back there!
AUBERON: But I only want a little chat. *(Sees GRAHAM and looks at his legs then says to GRAHAM)* Hm, nice tan.
GRAHAM: Minorca.
AUBERON: Minorca to you! *(Turns back to MIKE)* Now, let's see, what did you say your name is? *(They disappear the opposite side of the stage)*
MIKE: *(In ordinary voice)* Mike! *(Then again in a very deep voice)* Mike - the very macho disco king.
GRAHAM: *(To the GIRLS)* He's with the disco?
GIRLS: *(Together)* Yeah!
FELICITY: Both of them?
GIRLS: *(Together)* No! *(They giggle at one another)*
GRAHAM: Then - *(he is about to start again but realises it is useless)* I think I'll give this up! *(To FELICITY)*

Shall we play?

FELICITY: Why not? *(They start to set the net up)*

GRAHAM: *(Turning to GIRLS)* I wonder if you could just sit over there. *(He indicates the upstage left area, the GIRLS drag the chairs to where he has indicated)* Thank you. *(FELICITY and GRAHAM start to knock up)*

ALBERT: Oi! Oi! - what are you doing?

GRAHAM: Hullo Bert, just got to get this game in before the weekend, couldn't make it last night - commitments. *(He says this whilst he is playing so ALBERT is having to follow him around)*

ALBERT: *ALBERT* if you don't mind. You'll have to stop, you can't just come in here whenever you like, this floor takes hours to get clean, it was your lot's turn last night.

FELICITY: Yes but when we explained to Veronica she said it would be okay as there was nothing on tonight.

ALBERT: *(Advancing to FELICITY)* Our Veronica does not run this place, I do and there's nothing on tonight so that I can do my checks.

GRAHAM: It won't take long, Felicity isn't quite my standard - are you dear? *(To FELICITY)*

FELICITY: No, I suppose I am considerably better.

GRAHAM: Better? Only because your handicap is so high!

FELICITY: My handicap isn't high.

ALBERT: You'll have to stop - I won't have it!

GRAHAM: Your handicap is high pet!

FELICITY: It is not!

GRAHAM: It is!

FELICITY: It isn't! *(The shuttle is increasingly getting hit harder and harder)*

GRAHAM: Is!

FELICITY: Isn't!

GRAHAM: Is!

(ALBERT is attempting to catch the shuttle throughout this)

FELICITY: Never!

GRAHAM: Definitely!

FELICITY: No!

GRAHAM: Yes!

FELICITY: *(Stopping and coming to the net)* All right, I'll play you without a handicap. *(ALBERT is trying to intercede)*

GRAHAM: *(Coming to net)* Now that's silly!

FELICITY: Only because I'll beat you and then you'll have no excuse.

GRAHAM: I'll beat you anyway, but it's got to be fair. *(Passing under net)*

FELICITY: Fair for you to moan.

GRAHAM: I don't moan!

FELICITY: Yes you do! You're always moaning, if it isn't the net its the floor, or the lights, you've even complained about traffic noise!

GRAHAM: Well it can be very off-putting.

FELICITY: What! A bicycle going down the lane and ringing his bell!

GRAHAM: Incessantly.

FELICITY: Twice!

GRAHAM: It was more than twice.

FELICITY: It was twice!

GRAHAM: Well it was very loud and just at a crucial point.

FELICITY: It's always at a crucial point.

GRAHAM: Are you saying I cheat?

FELICITY: If the cap fits!

GRAHAM: I suppose you are as pure as the driven snow?

FELICITY: I'm just not devious that's all.

GRAHAM: Devious! *(he is shouting)* devious and a cheat, what next? I suppose I sabotage racquets and swap shuttles and why not throw in poison the tea?

FELICITY: Well you do only have orange juice.

GRAHAM: And you never try for advantage eh?

FELICITY: No!

GRAHAM: Well what about the sexy knickers you wear at finals and that gorgeous pink skirt *(his anger is subsiding)* and that loose bra *(he is softer)* and that lovely eye shadow, and that perfume and...and...*(They hold hands, look into each others eyes and say together)*

FELICITY & GRAHAM: The bike sheds!

(They dash off up stage left bumping ALBERT as they leave who almost sits on OTHER GIRL)

OTHER GIRL: Hey! *(ALBERT jumps forward and turns)*

ALBERT: Wha...Wha...

OTHER GIRL: You nearly sat on me!

ALBERT: Wha...Wha...*(He can't speak. MISS MANLEY enters up stage right)*

MANLEY: Mr. Standing, have you seen Auberon?

ALBERT: *(Spinning around)* Wha...Wha...

MANLEY: I can't find him anywhere. *(COXELEY enters up stage left)*

COXELEY: Albert can I continue please?

ALBERT: *(Spinning round)* Wha...Wha...

(MIKE and AUBERON appear through the curtain, MIKE backing being pursued by AUBERON)

AUBERON: It's a lovely boat, I usually moor it at Stratford, I'm sure you would like it. It has the most divine curtains. *(They cross down, ALBERT follows them with his gaze)*

MIKE: I really don't like boats. *(Still in a deep voice)*

AUBERON: Just say you'll take a look, you won't be disappointed.

MIKE: *(As they go off down right)* They make me sick, all that upping and downing, I mean the throbbing of the engine - No, I mean they're claustrophobic.

AUBERON: Oh yes, yes.

ALBERT: Wha...Wha...

(MISS MANLEY hurries after them down right)

MANLEY: Auberon, oh Auberon.

(The TWO GIRLS get up and move after them down right)

GHETTO GIRL: Mike are we gonna be long?

COXELEY: Where did I put that lectern? *(Exits up left. ALBERT is left alone on the stage, he backs off straight through the Badminton net. He disentangles himself and exits down right with net)*

ALBERT: Wha...Wha... *(COXELEY re-enters from up stage carrying the lectern. He restarts his address)*

COXELEY: Ladies and gentlemen, this evening in the short time allowed to me I would like to introduce you to the observations of a very new poet and philosopher - John Molesworthy Crudd - who said - you cannot make light of the darkness *(all the lights go out, there are shouts, squeals and various noises off stage, ALBERT appears on stage from up right with a torch)*

ALBERT: Stay still everyone, don't panic, I'll fix it! *(He walks straight into COXELEY. they fall over. The lights come back on and they are both on their knees staring at each other, a VOICE is heard from the wings)*

VOICE: Sorry, it's the electrician, the Town Hall said there was nothing on tonight so I decided to fix that faulty fuse, is Al the Caretaker about? *(ALBERT stands up, looks at COXELEY in disgust and storms into the wings)*

ALBERT: It's *Albert* to you! *(Off up left)*

(COXELEY stands and picks up the lectern, he begins his recital, during this MIKE and AUBERON enter up stage right, MIKE still backing, The TWO GIRLS follow chatting to each other, MISS MANLEY enters centre stage right talking to just about anyone who will listen and GRAHAM and FELICITY enter up stage left profusely apologising to each other)

(N.B. THE FOLLOWING PAGES ARE DIALOGUE WHICH, WHEN TIMED, WILL ALL FIT INTO THE PLAY, EACH SECTION IS ON INDIVIDUAL PAGES)

A

COXELEY: Atop the purple heather hill on high o-er
Dartmoors wind swept heights
On high above the Cornish crags and coves
and caves where wreckers lights
Would call a ship to loose her keel *(Enter MIKE and AUBERON) (B)*
To spill her cargo on the sand
On high
I stand
And misty eyed in face of wind *(Enter GIRLS) (C)*
I stare to West, to West the sun
her days work o-er dips low
The sky afire, aglow
I cry
The lonely tors my company
The winds my conversationalist *(Enter GRAHAM & FELICITY) (D)*
The birds my evening lullaby
The stars on high so high, so high
I cry
And with arched back my hands stretched high
Torment we mortals never more I cry *(Enter MISS MANLEY) (E)*
Night time is the artist of overeaction *(Enter ALBERT)*
Daytime the gallery of the obvious.

B

MIKE: It certainly sounds good and this pub always stays open late?

AUBERON: Always, the landlord is a personal friend and they're always looking for any person with a talent to entertain them.

MIKE: It's not a very polished act you understand, just a few jokes and impersonations.

AUBERON: Do you do female ones?

MIKE: A couple.

AUBERON: I bet they're good, who do you do?

MIKE: Danny La Rue, Hinge and Bracket, Edna Everage.

AUBERON: Oh you're a sauce, they're men!

MIKE: Are they? You say you met Elvis Presley?

AUBERON: Oh yes, charming young man, so much vitality and so good looking. I was doing excerpts from Romeo and Juliet in Hamberg, the theatre was his for the coming week, I just couldn't resist having a chat.

C

OTHER GIRL: He likes Cliff Richard.

GHETTO GIRL: He doesn't.

OTHER GIRL: And he keeps goin' on about someone called Dennis Lotus.

GHETTO GIRL: Who?

OTHER GIRL: I know, they must be dead, half of 'em. Last night we were watchin' telly and he suddenly said to me mum Alma Cogan used to have frocks like that. I said who? Alma Cogan he said. Who's she? I said, then he just went into a sort of dream.

GHETTO GIRL: I know, mine's the same, only with football. All he can ever say is don't know what's it's like to feel a lace on the head, or, we used to have proper boots in our days and then *Substitutes* and he shakes his head. *(Pause)*

OTHER GIRL: Our Garry's playin' again on Sunday, shall we go for a giggle?

GHETTO GIRL: Will Steve be playin'?

OTHER GIRL: How do I know. Probably.

GHETTO GIRL: Well I might then.

OTHER GIRL: Oh don't force yerself.

D

GRAHAM: I'm sorry Felicity, it's just that you inflame me so much.

FELICITY: That's all right Graham, but you must stop trying to be so domineering, it really isn't you.

GRAHAM: No I know but I just want to assert myself, yet every time I try it's the wrong place and all the wrong words come out.

FELICITY: You must just relax and be yourself.

GRAHAM: I will.

FELICITY: And next time June calls you a burk, ignore her.

GRAHAM: I will.

FELICITY: And if Giles calls you your Royal Wetness, don't sulk, just laugh.

GRAHAM: I will.

FELICITY: And if Mary tells you to make the tea again because it saves you sitting round, tell her you've brought a flask.

GRAHAM: I haven't got a flask.

FELICITY: Lie!

GRAHAM: I will.

FELICITY: And if Peter asks you what you've been doing with his wife - panic!

GRAHAM: I will - Peter! God he doesn't know does he?

FELICITY: Calm down, he's still in Singapore.

E

MISS MANLEY: *(Pacing about the stage, turning and facing the podium)* We may need to extend the stage a little *(walking up stage and looking up)* and we'll probably have to fit a further lighting batten. The curtains will easily rehang forward of their present position but I must check that they open and close easily. Don't want any embarrassing moments changing scenes. What do you think about scenes Auberon? Simple or elaborate? I think simple is best considering the storage space available and the fact that we only have five back stage, still the actors can help if they're not in costume or helping with the tea and biscuits. Do we need any sound Auberon, I mean crowd scenes, etc, off stage noise, you know, Oh and what about make-up, who can do make-up?

ALBERT: *(Entering centre stage left)* Shut up! All of you, shut up! *(They slowly quieten)* Now get out! Go away! There is nothing on tonight! Get out!

(With muttered 'very well's', etc, they all leave, ALBERT sits in one of the chairs and mops his brow. There is a period of quiet. A voice is heard from the podium)

VERONICA: Shan't be long, just wait there a minute. *(She pokes her head through the curtains)* Oh good, nothing on. *(She turns in the podium)* It's okay, there's no-one here. *(She talks forward again)* Daddy, I know you won't mind but as there's nothing on tonight I told A-kay-la she could hold her cubs five a side finals tonight, that's okay isn't it? *(She turns to podium again)* All right A-kay-la, bring them in, there's only Daddy and he's glad of something to do.

ALBERT: *(Rising and turning up stage with rising voice)* Veronica. *(He moves towards her centre)*
(CURTAIN CALL - Curtain open and GRAHAM and FELICITY cross to down right, bow. MIKE and GIRLS cross to down left, bow. COXELEY crosses to down right inside of

FELICITY, bow. AUBERON and MANLEY through curtain, down centre, bow. All bow. ALBERT appears up centre with brush, sees everyone is back) What's this? I thought I told you lot to clear off. *(He shoos them off with his brush. Continues to sweep stage. VERONICA appears down right, crosses halfway to ALBERT)*

VERONICA: Daddy...

ALBERT: *(Turns, sees her)* Veronica! *(Attempts to sweep her up with brush as he chases her off)*

FINAL CURTAIN

PROPERTIES

Music stand/lectern
2 Badminton Racquets
4 Shuttlecocks
1 Imitation Badminton Net 9'0 long x 5'0 high.
1 Plastic coated Foam Mat 2'6 x 6'0
1 Cassette Tape Player with tape of loud music
1 Torch
1 Soft sweeping brush
1 Sports bag
1 Towel
1 Sweeping brush

(Badminton net and stands - Two heavy broom handles slotte into two 12 inch square bases which are weighted wit approximately 4lb in weight in each. 10ft of netting by 3f deep attached to string top and bottom and then attached t poles)

LIGHTING

Stage	4 x 500w flood
F.O.H.	2 x 500w white spots centre
	2 x 500w amber spots, left and right

LIGHTING PLOT

Page ( ) "Whether tis nobler" Auberon.
All lights out. 2 seconds back on.

NOTHING ON TONIGHT

Page ( ) "Till it be morrow" Auberon.
Lights flash on and off 3 seconds.
Page ( ) "You cannot make light of the darkness" Coxeley.
All lights out.
Page ( ) "Don't panic I'll fix it" Albert.
5 seconds, all lights on.

SOUND

Page ( ) "The slings and arrows" Auberon.
Banging back stage.
Page ( ) "Outrageous fortune" Auberon.
Toilet flush over system.
Page ( ) "Rude of you" Miss Manley.
Thumping back stage.